DEPARTMENT OF THE NAVY
OFFICE OF THE SECRETARY
1000 NAVY PENTAGON
WASHINGTON, D.C. 20350-1000

SECNAVINST 6320.24A
BUMED-03L
16 February 1999

SECNAV INSTRUCTION 6320.24A

From: Secretary of the Navy
To: All Ships and Stations

Subj: MENTAL HEALTH EVALUATIONS OF MEMBERS OF THE ARMED
       FORCES

Ref: (a) DoD Directive 6490.1, "Mental Health Evaluations of
           Members of the Armed Forces," of 1 Oct 97 (NOTAL)
       (b) Public Law 102-484 "National Defense Authorization Act
           for Fiscal Year 1993," of 23 Oct 92
       (c) DoD Directive 7050.6, "Military Whistleblower
           Protection," of 12 Aug 95 (NOTAL)
       (d) National Center for State Courts' Guidelines For
           Involuntary Civil Commitment, 1986 (NOTAL)
       (e) American Psychiatric Association's Task Force Report,
           "Involuntary Commitment to Outpatient Treatment,"
           1987[1]
       (f) American Psychiatric Association, "Guidelines for
           Legislation on the Psychiatric Hospitalization of
           Adults," American Journal of Psychiatry, 140:5, May
           83 (NOTAL)
       (g) American Psychiatric Association, "The Principles of
           Medical Ethics with Annotations Especially Applicable
           to Psychiatry," 1995[1]
       (h) American Psychological Association, "Ethical
           Principles of Psychologists and Code of Conduct,"
           1992[2]
       (i) National Association of Social Workers' "Code of
           Ethics," 1996[3]
       (j) Chapter 47, of Title 10, U.S. Code, "Uniform Code of
           Military Justice," (UCMJ)
       (k) DoD Directive 6400.1, "Family Advocacy Program
           (FAP)," 23 Jun 92 (NOTAL)
       (l) DoD Directive 1010.4, "Alcohol and Drug Abuse by DoD
           Personnel," 3 Sep 97 (NOTAL)
       (m) DoD Instruction 1010.6, "Rehabilitation and Referral
           Services for Alcohol and Drug Abusers," 13 Mar 85
           (NOTAL)
       (n) DoD Directive 6040.37, "Confidentiality of Medical
           Quality Assurance (QA) Records," 9 Jul 96 (NOTAL)

---

[1] Available from the American Psychiatric Association, 1400 K Street, NW, Washington, DC 20005

[2] Available from the American Psychological Association, 750 First Street, NE, Washington, DC 20002

[3] Available from the National Association of Social Workers, 750 First Street, NE, Suite 700, Washington, DC 20002

SECNAVINST 6320.24A

(o) Section 1102 of Title 10, U.S. Code
(p) American Psychiatric Association (APA), "Diagnostic
    and Statistical Manual of Mental Disorders,"
    (DSM-IV), Fourth Edition, Washington, DC, APA
    Press, 1994
(q) SECNAVINST 1730.7A, "Religious Ministries Within the
    Department of the Navy" (NOTAL)

Encl: (1) Definitions
      (2) Sample Letter, Commanding Officer Request for Routine
          (Non-emergency) Mental Health Evaluation
      (3) Sample Letter, Service Member Notification of
          Commanding Officer Referral for Mental Health
          Evaluation
      (4) Sample Letter From Mental Health Care Provider to
          Service Member's Commanding Officer
      (5) Guidelines for Mental Health Evaluation for Imminent
          Dangerousness

1. Purpose

    a. To issue Department of Navy (DON) policy, assign
responsibility, and prescribe procedures per reference (a) for
the referral, evaluation, treatment and administrative management
of service members who are directed by their commands for mental
health evaluation and/or assessment of risk for potentially
dangerous behavior. This instruction is a complete revision and
should be reviewed in its entirety.

    b. To establish the rights of service members referred by
their commands for mental health evaluations.

    c. To establish procedures for outpatient and inpatient
mental health evaluations that will provide protection to members
referred by their commands for such evaluations.

    d. To prohibit the use of mental health evaluation referrals
by commands in reprisal against whistle blowers for disclosures
protected by references (a) through (c).

    e. To provide guidance to mental health care providers and
commanding officers on evaluation, treatment, and administrative
management of service members who may suffer from serious mental
disorders and who may be imminently or potentially dangerous.

2

f. To establish procedures for the psychiatric hospitalization of active duty service members modeled after guidelines prepared by professional civilian mental health organizations for psychiatric hospitalization and treatment of adults, per references (d) through (q).

2. Cancellation. SECNAVINST 6320.24.

3. Background

a. Military members play an important role in maintaining accountability and responsibility in Government and should be encouraged to come forward with information that may ultimately help to improve the function of Government, including the DON. They should not be subjected to unwarranted mental health evaluations or involuntary hospitalization as a form of harassment or in retaliation for revealing flaws within the DON. Regardless of the reason for the referral or hospitalization, such decisions must be based upon objective standards. Service members must not be arbitrarily subjected to mental health evaluations.

b. Service members determined to be imminently or potentially dangerous pose a heightened risk to themselves and to others. Commanding officers and mental health professionals must recognize this risk and take appropriate action to ensure the safety of the service member and others.

4. Applicability

a. This instruction applies to: all DON civilian employees, active duty military personnel (both Regular and Reserve), special Government employees, personnel of non-appropriated fund activities, and midshipmen of the U.S. Naval Academy. This instruction also pertains to officers and enlisted personnel of the inactive U.S. Naval and Marine Corps Reserve on active duty for training, and other persons performing duties for the DON employed within military treatment facilities (i.e., Public Health Service personnel and contract employees).

b. This instruction does not apply to voluntary self-referrals; diagnostic referrals requested by non-mental health care providers not part of the service member's chain of command as a matter of independent clinical judgment and when the service member consents to the evaluation; responsibility and competency inquiries conducted under the Rule for Court Martial 706 of the Manual for Courts-Martial; interviews conducted under the Family Advocacy Program; interviews conducted under drug or alcohol abuse rehabilitation programs; and evaluations expressly required by applicable Service regulation for special duties or occupational classifications.

5. Definitions. See enclosure (1).

6. DON Policy

   a. Commanding officers and officers in charge (hereafter referred to as COs), when practicable, shall consult with a mental health provider prior to referring a service member for a mental health evaluation.

   b. A service member shall be afforded the rights and protections accorded by references (a) and (b) and this instruction when referred for mental health evaluation.

   c. No person shall refer a service member for a mental health evaluation as a reprisal for making or preparing a lawful communication to a Member of Congress, any appropriate authority in the chain of command of the member, an inspector general (IG), or a member of a DoD audit, inspection, investigation, or law enforcement organization.

   d. No person shall restrict a service member from lawfully communicating with an IG, attorney, Member of Congress, chaplain, or others about the service member's referral for a mental health evaluation.

   e. Mental health care providers shall provide COs timely information concerning service members referred for mental health evaluations. At a minimum, that information will include: diagnosis; treatment recommendations; and administrative management recommendations.

   f. Nothing in this instruction shall be construed to limit the authority of COs to refer a service member for emergency mental health evaluation or treatment when circumstances suggest the need for such action.

   g. Upon request by a service member for advice from an attorney, an attorney who is a member of the Armed Forces or employed by the Department of Defense shall be appointed at no cost to the service member to advise the service member. If a military attorney is not reasonably available, every effort should be made to provide legal consultation by telephone.

7. Enforceability

a. Violation of paragraph 6c or 6d by any person subject to reference (j) is punishable as a violation of the Uniform Code of Military Justice (UCMJ), Article 92 (Violation of a Lawful General Regulation).

b. Violation of paragraphs 6c or 6d by civilian employees is punishable under regulations governing civilian disciplinary or adverse actions.

c. Failure to comply with other provisions of this instruction shall be addressed through appropriate action.

8. Procedures

a. Non-emergency Mental Health Evaluation Referrals

(1) Commanding Officer Actions

(a) The responsibility for determining whether a referral for mental health evaluation should be made rests with the service member's designated CO at the time of referral. This authority may not be delegated.

(b) When a CO determines it is necessary to direct a service member for mental health evaluation, the CO first shall consult with a mental health care provider to discuss the service member's actions and behaviors. The mental health care provider shall provide advice and recommendations about whether an evaluation should be conducted, and whether any needed evaluation should be done on a routine or an emergency basis. If a mental health care provider is not available, the CO shall consult a physician, if available, or the senior privileged non-physician provider present. For non-emergency referrals, the CO shall forward to the CO of the medical treatment facility (MTF) or clinic a letter, formally requesting a mental health evaluation. (See enclosure (2).)

(c) COs of MTFs or clinics who wish to refer a service member for a non-emergency mental health evaluation shall forward to the director of that mental health department a letter formally requesting a mental health evaluation. (See enclosure (2)).

(d) The service member's CO shall ensure the service member is provided a written letter, per enclosure (3), at least two business days before a non-emergency referral for mental health evaluation. This letter shall include, at a minimum, the following:

<u>1</u>. A brief factual description of the behaviors and/or verbal communications that led to the CO's decision to refer the service member for mental health evaluation.

<u>2</u>. The name of the mental health care provider with whom the CO consulted before making the referral. If a consultation with a mental health care provider was not possible, the letter shall state the reasons why.

<u>3</u>. Notification of the service member's rights per reference (b) and enclosure (3).

<u>4</u>. The date, time, and place the mental health evaluation is scheduled and the name and grade or rate of the mental health care provider who will conduct the evaluation.

<u>5</u>. The titles and telephone numbers of other authorities, including attorneys, IGs, and chaplains, who can assist a service member who questions the necessity of the referral.

<u>6</u>. The name and signature of the CO.

(e) Service members shall acknowledge having been advised of the reasons for the mental health referral and acknowledge having been advised of their rights by signing the letters. If service members refuse to sign, the CO shall note the refusals on the letters, in addition to any reasons service members may have given for not signing.

(f) Copies of the signed letters shall be provided to service members and to the mental health care providers who will conduct the evaluations.

(g) Service members may not waive their right to receive the written letters and statements of rights described above in subparagraph 8a(1)(d).

(2) Mental Health Care Provider Action

(a) Before a non-emergency mental health evaluation occurs, the mental health care provider shall determine if procedures for referral for mental health evaluation have been followed per reference (a) and this instruction. The mental health care provider shall review the signed letter, including the Statement of Service Member's Rights forwarded by the service member's CO.

(b) Whenever there is evidence that indicates the mental health evaluation may have been requested improperly, the mental health care provider shall first confer with the referring command to clarify issues about the process and procedures used in referring the service member. If, after such discussion, the mental health care provider believes the referral may have been conducted improperly, per references (a) through (c) and this instruction, the mental health care provider shall report such evidence through his or her chain of command to the next higher level of the referring CO.

(c) The mental health care provider shall advise the service member referred for mental health evaluation of the purpose, nature, and likely consequences of the evaluation before the evaluation begins, and shall advise the service member the evaluation is not confidential.

(d) Absent an emergency, when a mental health care provider both evaluates and provides therapy to a service member referred by the service member's CO, the possible conflict of duties should be explained clearly to the service member at the beginning of the therapeutic relationship. (See Section 4 of reference (g); Principle B (Integrity), Principle D (Respect for People's Rights and Dignity), and Principle E (Concern for Other's Welfare) of reference (h); and Principles of Dignity and Worth of the Person, Importance of Human Relationships, and Integrity of reference (i).)

(e) Following evaluation, the mental health care provider shall forward a letter to the service member's CO to inform the CO of the results of the mental health evaluation and provide recommendations, see enclosure (4). (See also paragraph 8(g) for those service members evaluated as imminently or potentially dangerous.)

b. Emergency Evaluations

(1) CO Actions

(a) When the CO makes a clear and reasoned judgment the service member's situation constitutes an emergency, the CO's first priority shall be to protect the Service member and others from harm.

(b) The CO shall make every effort to consult a mental health care provider, or other privileged health care provider if a mental health care provider is not readily available, prior to referring or sending a service member for an emergency mental health evaluation.

(c) The CO shall safely convey the service member to the nearest mental health care provider or, if unavailable, a physician, or the senior privileged non physician provider present, as soon as is practicable.

(d) If, due to the nature of the emergency, the CO was unable to consult with a mental health care provider or other privileged health care provider, the CO shall forward a letter documenting the circumstances and observations of the service member that led to the CO's decision to refer the service member on an emergency basis. This letter shall be forwarded by facsimile, overnight mail or courier to the treating health care provider as soon as is practicable.

(e) The CO shall, as soon as is practicable, provide the service member a letter and statement of rights as described in subparagraph 8(a)(1)(d).

(2) Mental Health Care Provider Actions

(a) Before an emergency mental health evaluation occurs, the mental health care provider shall determine if procedures for referral for emergency mental health evaluations have been followed using the guidelines of this instruction.

(b) Whenever there is evidence which indicates the mental health evaluation may have been requested improperly, the mental health care provider shall first confer with the referring command to clarify issues about the process and procedures used in referring the service member. If, after such discussion, the mental health care provider believes the referral may have been conducted improperly, per references (a) through (c) and this instruction, the mental health care provider shall report such evidence through his or her chain of command to the next higher level of the referring CO. The provider will not delay the evaluation, regardless of procedural concerns.

(c) The mental health care provider shall advise the service member referred for mental health evaluation of the purpose, nature, and likely consequences of the evaluation before the evaluation begins, and shall advise the service member that the evaluation is not confidential.

(d) Following the evaluation, the mental health care provider shall forward a letter to the service member's CO to inform him or her of the results of the mental health evaluation and provide recommendations, see enclosure (4). (See paragraph 8(g) for service members evaluated as imminently or potentially dangerous.)

c. Involuntary Hospitalization for Psychiatric Evaluation and/or Treatment

(1) An involuntary hospital admission is appropriate only when a provider, privileged to admit psychiatric patients, makes a reasoned, good faith clinical judgment the service member has, or likely has, a severe mental disorder and poses a danger to himself or herself or others, so the evaluation or treatment cannot reasonably be provided by a less restrictive level of care or when less intensive treatments would result in inadequate medical care. Hospitalization is appropriate only when consistent with the least restrictive alternative principle as described in reference (h), and defined in enclosure (2).

(2) COs shall coordinate with health care providers, as soon after admission as the service member's condition permits, to inform the service member of the reasons for his or her admission, the likely consequence(s) of the evaluation and any treatment, and the service member's rights.

(3) The service member shall have the right to contact a relative, friend, chaplain, attorney, and/or an IG as soon after admission as the service member's condition permits.

(4) The service member shall be evaluated by the attending privileged psychiatrist, or another privileged physician if a psychiatrist is not available, within 24 hours

9

after admission to determine if continued hospitalization and/or treatment is clinically indicated or, alternately, to determine if the service member should be discharged from the hospital.

(5) If the attending privileged psychiatrist, or another privileged physician if a psychiatrist is not available, determines continued hospitalization is clinically indicated, the service member shall be notified orally and in writing of the reasons for continued hospitalization.

(6) Independent Review Requirement

(a) Within 72 hours of admission, an independent, privileged psychiatrist, or other medical officer, if a psychiatrist is not available, shall review the factors that led to the involuntary admission and shall assess the clinical appropriateness of continued involuntary hospitalization. The reviewer shall not be in the member's immediate chain of command, shall be an O4 or greater (or civilian equivalent), and shall be an impartial, disinterested party appointed by the medical treatment facility CO.

(b) The review procedure shall include a review of the medical record, referral letter, and an examination of the service member.

(c) The reviewer shall notify the service member of the right to have legal representation during the review by a judge advocate or by an attorney of the service member's choosing, at the service member's own expense, if reasonably available.

(d) The reviewer shall introduce himself/herself to the service member, indicate the reasons for the interview, and indicate he or she shall conduct an independent, impartial review of the reasons for the service member's involuntary psychiatric hospitalization.

(e) The reviewer shall determine and document in the inpatient medical record whether continued involuntary psychiatric hospitalization and/or treatment is clinically appropriate. If indicated, the reviewer shall specify the clinical conditions for continued involuntary inpatient treatment; the clinical conditions required for discharge from the hospital; and shall determine when the next independent review for continued involuntary hospitalization shall occur. (Independent reviews must be done at least every five business days.) The service member shall be notified of the reviewer's recommendations and the date of the next review.

(f) The reviewer shall determine if proper procedures for the mental health referral were followed. Whenever there is evidence which indicates the mental health evaluation may have been requested or conducted improperly, the reviewer shall first confer with the referring command and the admitting mental health care provider to clarify issues about the process or procedures used in referring and/or admitting the service member. If the reviewer determines the referral or admission was made improperly, the reviewer shall report the finding through his or her chain of command to the next level above the referring commanding officer or admitting physician for further investigation and for possible referral to the DON IG or the DoD IG.

d. Special Procedures for Imminently or Potentially Dangerous Service members

(1) CO Actions

(a) A CO shall refer a service member for an emergency mental health evaluation as soon as is practicable whenever a service member, by actions or words, intends or is likely to cause serious injury to himself, herself or others and when the facts and circumstances indicate the service member possesses the ability to cause such injury and when the CO believes the service member may be suffering from a serious mental disorder. Prior to such referral, the CO shall attempt to consult with a mental health care provider, or other health care provider, if a mental health care provider is not available.

(b) COs shall consider information and recommendations about service members provided by social workers or other DoD personnel assigned duties under the Family Advocacy Program, operated under the authority of reference (k), or the rehabilitation and referral programs for alcohol and drug abusers, operated under the authority of reference (l) and reference (m).

(c) Only DoD psychiatrists, doctoral level clinical psychologists or doctoral level clinical social workers with clinical practice privileges have authority to clinically

11

evaluate a risk for imminent dangerousness. Only these providers may perform mental health evaluations of service members identified within the scope of this subsection.

(d) Other privileged health care providers frequently perform routine clinical evaluations of service members in which assessment of potential dangerousness may be an element. This instruction does not restrict such evaluations.

(e) Whenever a privileged health care provider concludes, in the course of a mental health evaluation, that a service member may be imminently dangerous, the health care provider shall refer the service member to a privileged, doctoral level mental health care provider for evaluation and assessment of risk for imminent dangerousness.

(f) In those rare instances in which a privileged doctoral level mental health care provider is not readily available, a CO may refer a service member, who the commanding officer suspects is imminently dangerous, to a physician, if available, or to the senior privileged non-physician provider present for initial evaluation, pending subsequent evaluation by a privileged doctoral level mental health care provider.

e. Requirements for Conducting Emergency Mental Health Evaluations for Imminent Dangerousness

(1) Emergency evaluations of service members believed to be imminently dangerous shall be conducted as soon as possible, but within 24 hours of the initial request. Meanwhile, the CO shall take action to protect the service member's safety and the safety of others.

(2) Mental health evaluations shall be conducted in a manner consistent with applicable clinical standards of care, as supplemented by enclosure (5). Such evaluations shall include a detailed patient history, a mental status examination, laboratory studies, and, to the extent clinically indicated, a physical and neurological examination.

(3) In cases in which a mental health evaluation is indicated, and there is a clear and reasonable basis to conclude the service member may be suffering from a serious mental disorder, and the service member is judged to be or may become imminently dangerous, and a complete and thorough evaluation cannot be conducted as an outpatient within an acceptable time

period (usually less than 24 hours), the service member may be admitted to a psychiatric unit (or medical unit, if a psychiatric unit is not available) for an inpatient evaluation.

(4) The decision to admit a service member for an inpatient mental health evaluation or treatment rests solely with a mental health care provider who has approved hospital admitting privileges. In cases of deployed units, or isolated geographic locations where no mental health care providers are available, a physician, if available, or the senior privileged non-physician provider present, shall take actions and/or make recommendations to the service member's CO to protect the service member's safety and that of others, until such an evaluation can be conducted.

(5) When a mental health care provider performs a comprehensive mental health evaluation and determines a service member is at significantly increased risk of imminently or potentially dangerous behavior, the provider also shall take precautions, contained in reference (a) and this instruction.

(6) The responsible privileged health care provider shall document in the medical record the clinical assessment, including the assessment of risk for imminent dangerousness, treatment plan, progress of treatment, discharge assessment, recommendations to COs, and any notification of potential victims as required by reference (a), subparagraph D7 and this instruction.

f. Health Care Providers Duty to Take Precautions Against Threatened Injury

(1) In any case in which a service member has communicated to a health care provider with clinical practice privileges an explicit threat to kill or seriously injure a clearly identified or reasonably identifiable person, or to destroy property under circumstances likely to lead to serious bodily injury or death, and the service member has the apparent intent and ability to carry out the threat, the provider shall take precautions against such threatened injury. Such precautions may include any of the following:

(a) Notification of the service member's CO that the service member is imminently or potentially dangerous.

(b) Notification of the military and/or civilian law enforcement authority where the threatened injury may occur.

(c) Notification of any identified potential victim(s) of the threats made.

(d) Recommendation to the service member's CO that appropriate precautions be taken.

(e) Admitting the service member to an inpatient psychiatric or medical ward for evaluation and/or treatment of a mental disorder.

(f) Referral of the service member's case to the Service's physical evaluation board per reference (a), subparagraph D6c(1).

(g) Recommendation to the CO the service member be administratively separated for personality disorder per reference (a), subparagraph D6c(2) or other applicable separation authority.

(2) Prior to discharge of an imminently or potentially dangerous service member from inpatient status, a health care provider shall notify the service member's CO, and any identifiable individuals who may be at risk of serious injury from the service member, about the service member's pending discharge.

(3) The health care provider shall document in the medical record the date, time and name of each person and agency contacted when taking precautions against threatened injury.

(4) The health care provider shall inform the service member these precautions have been taken.

g. Recommendations to COs

(1) Upon completion of a mental health examination of an imminently or potentially dangerous service member, the mental health care provider shall immediately provide to the service member's CO a letter that shall address at a minimum the diagnosis, prognosis, treatment plan, and recommendations regarding fitness and suitability for continued service and shall

14

make recommendations for precaution(s), if appropriate, and administrative management of the service member. (See reference (a) subparagraph D6, and enclosures (4) and (5) of this instruction.)

(2) The mental health care provider shall review with the service member the clinical summaries, letter, and recommendations made to the CO.

h. Actions by COs

(1) Whenever a privileged mental health care provider makes a recommendation to the service member's CO on an imminently or potentially dangerous service member, the CO shall make a written record of the actions taken and reasons therefore.

(2) Whenever a mental health care provider recommends to a service member's CO the member be separated from military service due to a personality disorder and imminently or potentially dangerous behavior, that recommendation shall be co-signed by the mental health care provider's CO. If the service member's CO declines to follow the recommendation(s) of the provider, the service member's CO shall forward a letter to his or her immediate superior in the chain of command within two business days of receiving the recommendation(s), explaining the decision to retain the service member against medical advice.

i. Medical Quality Management Case Review

(1) Every mental health evaluation or treatment case in which a service member ultimately commits an act resulting in suicide, homicide, serious injury or significant violence, shall be systematically reviewed per the MTF's plan for improving patient care and health outcomes. Assessment of findings shall be used to design and measure improvements of patient care processes, risk-management, and MTF staff competence.

(2) Reviews shall focus particularly on clinical assessment, treatment, progress, administrative recommendations and administrative follow-through, as documented in the medical and personnel records.

(3) Case reviews shall be included in ongoing quality management activities. Such reviews shall include lessons learned and recommendations for improvement in the future medical management of service members at increased risk of dangerous behavior.

15

    (4) Medical quality management case review activities shall be coordinated as appropriate with other Service investigations.

    (5) Medical quality management case review records shall be confidential per references (n) and (o).

9. Responsibilities

    a. The Chief of Naval Operations and Commandant of the Marine Corps shall:

    (1) Ensure COs follow the requirements of the pertinent DoD and Service directives, instructions and regulations for the management of imminently or potentially dangerous service members and the procedures for proper referral of those service members for mental health evaluations.

    (2) Ensure COs consider recommendations made by mental health care providers in cases involving imminently or potentially dangerous service members and ensure they take necessary precautions to appropriately manage those service members.

    (3) Ensure mental health care providers follow the requirements of the pertinent DoD and Service directives, instructions and regulations for the management of imminently or potentially dangerous service members.

    (4) Ensure appropriate periodic training is conducted for all DON service members and civilian employees in the initial management and referral of service members who are believed to be imminently dangerous. Such training shall include the recognition of potentially dangerous behaviors; appropriate security responses to emergency situations; and administrative management of such cases. Training shall be specific to the needs, grade or rate, level of responsibility and assignment of the service member or civilian employee.

    b. The DON IG shall:

    (1) Report to the DoD IG, within ten working days of receipt, all allegations submitted by the service member or the service member's legal guardian to the DON IG, a service member was referred for a mental health evaluation in violation of this instruction. The notification shall be made in writing and shall include the following:

   (a) Grade or rate, name and duty location of the service member.

   (b) Synopsis of the specific allegation(s) and the data received by the IG.

   (c) Grade or rate, name, and duty location of the proposed investigator.

   (2) Unless notified the DoD IG assumes investigative responsibility for a particular matter, initiate or cause to be initiated, an investigation of the issues raised in the allegation(s).

   (3) If the investigation is not completed within 90 days of receipt of an allegation, provide an interim report to the DoD IG on the 90th day and supplement it every 60 days thereafter, until the final report is submitted.

   (4) Provide the DoD IG, a copy of the final report of investigation with attachments within one week of completion of the final report of investigation.

   (5) Provide to the DoD IG, a written report of any disciplinary and/or administrative action, and the nature thereof, taken against any individual in connection with the investigation, within one week after such action is taken.

10. Reports. The reporting requirements contained in this instruction are exempt from reports control by SECNAVINST 5214.2B.

Jerry MacArthur Hultin
Under Secretary of the Navy

Distribution:
SNDL Parts 1 and 2
MARCORPS PCN 71000000000 and 71000000100

DEFINITIONS

1. Emergency. A situation in which a service member is threatening, by words or actions, to imminently cause harm to himself or herself, or to imminently destroy property under circumstances likely to lead to serious personal injury or death and where delaying a mental health evaluation could endanger the service member or others. An emergency may also be construed to mean an inability by the individual to care for himself or herself to the extent that delaying a mental health evaluation could endanger the life of the service member.

2. Imminent Dangerousness. A clinical finding or judgment by a privileged, doctoral level mental health care provider, based upon a comprehensive mental health evaluation, an individual is at substantial risk of committing an act in the near future which would result in serious injury to himself or herself or another person, or would destroy property under circumstances likely to lead to serious injury, and the individual manifests the intent and ability to carry out that action. A violent act of a sexual nature is considered an act which would result in serious personal injury.

3. Inspector General (IG). The Inspector General, DoD, and a military or civilian employee assigned or detailed under DoD component regulations to serve as an IG at any command level in one of the DoD components.

4. Least Restrictive Alternative Principle. A principle under which a member of the Armed Forces committed for hospitalization and treatment shall be placed in the most appropriate and therapeutically available setting that is no more restrictive than is conducive to the most effective form of treatment, and in which treatment is available and the risk of physical injury and/or property damage posed by such a placement are warranted by the proposed plan of treatment.

5. Mental Disorder. As defined by reference (p), a mental disorder is:

> A clinically significant behavioral or psychological syndrome or pattern that occurs in an individual and is associated with present distress (e.g., a painful symptom) or disability (e.g., impairment in one or more

important areas of functioning) or with a
significantly increased risk of suffering
death, pain, disability, or an important loss
of freedom. In addition, this syndrome or
pattern must not be merely an expectable and
culturally sanctioned response to a
particular event; for example, the death of a
loved one. Whatever its original cause, it
must currently be considered a manifestation
of a behavioral, psychological, or biological
dysfunction in the individual. Neither
deviant behavior (e.g., political, religious,
or sexual) nor conflicts that are primarily
between the individual and society are mental
disorders unless the deviance or conflict is
a symptom of a dysfunction in the individual,
as described above.

6. <u>Mental Health Evaluation</u>. A clinical assessment of a service
member for a mental, physical, or personality disorder, the
purpose of which is to determine a service member's clinical
mental health status and/or fitness and/or suitability for
Service. The mental health evaluation shall consist of, at a
minimum, a clinical interview and mental status examination and
may include, additionally: a review of medical records; a review
of other records, such as the Service personnel record;
information forwarded by the service member's CO; psychological
testing; physical examination; and laboratory and/or other
specialized testing. Interviews conducted by the Family Advocacy
Program or the Service's Drug and Alcohol Abuse Rehabilitation
Program personnel are not considered mental health evaluations
for the purpose of this instruction.

7. <u>Mental Health Care Provider</u>. A psychiatrist, doctoral level
clinical psychologist or doctoral level clinical social worker
with necessary and appropriate professional credentials who is
privileged to conduct mental health evaluations for DoD
components.

8. <u>Potentially Dangerous (Not Imminently Dangerous)</u>. A clinical
finding or judgment by a privileged, doctoral level mental health
care provider, based on a comprehensive mental health
evaluation, an individual has demonstrated violent behavior
against himself or herself or another person, or of destroying
property under circumstances likely to lead to serious personal

injury or death, or possesses longstanding character traits indicating a tendency towards such violence, but is not currently immediately dangerous to himself, herself or to others. A violent act of a sexual nature is considered an act which would result in serious personal injury.

9. <u>Protected Communication</u>. Any lawful communication to a Member of Congress or an IG. A communication in which a member of the Armed Forces communicates information the member reasonably believes evidences a violation of law or regulation, including sexual harassment or unlawful discrimination, mismanagement, a gross waste of funds or other resources, an abuse of authority, or a substantial and specific danger to public health or safety when such communication is made to any of the following: A Member of Congress; an IG; a member of a DoD audit, inspection, investigation, or law enforcement organization; or any other person or organization (including any person or organization in the chain of command) designated under DoD component regulations or other established administrative procedures to receive such communication.

10. <u>Self-Referral (or Voluntary Referral)</u>. The process of seeking information about or obtaining an appointment for a mental health evaluation or treatment independently initiated by a service member.

11. <u>Senior Privileged Nonphysician Provider</u>. In the absence of a physician, the most experienced and trained health care provider who holds privileges to evaluate and treat patients, such as a clinical social worker, a nurse practitioner, an independent duty corpsman, etc.

SAMPLE LETTER

COMMANDING OFFICER REQUEST FOR ROUTINE
(NONEMERGENCY) MENTAL HEALTH EVALUATION

FOR OFFICIAL USE ONLY

6320
Ser
Date

From: Commanding Officer, (Name of Command)
To: Commanding Officer, (Name of medical treatment facility
       or clinic)

Subj: COMMAND REFERRAL FOR MENTAL HEALTH EVALUATION OF (SERVICE
       MEMBER RANK, NAME, BRANCH OF SERVICE AND SSN)

Ref: (a) DoD Directive 6490.1, "Mental Health Evaluations of
           Members of the Armed Forces," 1 Oct 97 (NOTAL)
       (b) SECNAV Instruction 6320.24A, "Mental Health
           Evaluations of Members of the Armed Forces,"
       (c) Section 546 of Public Law 102-484, "National Defense
           Authorization Act for Fiscal Year 1993," Oct 1992
       (d) DoD Directive 7050.6, "Military Whistleblower
           Protection," 12 Aug 95 (NOTAL)

Encl: (1) My ltr (SSIC, serial #, date)

1. Per references (a) through (d), I hereby request a formal
mental health evaluation of (rank and name of service member).

2. (Name and rank of service member) has (years) and (months)
active duty Service and has been assigned to my command since
(date). Armed Services Vocational Aptitude Battery scores upon
enlistment were: (list scores). Past average performance marks
have ranged from _____ to _____ (give numerical scores). Legal
action is/is not currently pending against the service member.
(If charges are pending, list dates and UCMJ articles). Past
legal actions include: (List dates, charges, nonjudicial
punishments and/or findings of Courts Martial.)

FOR OFFICIAL USE ONLY

Enclosure (2)

SECNAVINST 6320.24A
18 FEB 1999

Subj: COMMAND REFERRAL FOR MENTAL HEALTH EVALUATION OF (SERVICE
       MEMBER RANK, NAME, BRANCH OF SERVICE AND SSN)

3. I have forwarded to the service member a letter that
advises (rank and name of service member) of his (or her) rights.
This letter also states the reasons for this referral, the name
of the mental health care provider(s) with whom I consulted,
and the names and telephone numbers of judge advocates, DoD
attorneys and/or Inspectors General who may advise and assist him
(or her). A copy of this letter, enclosure (1), is attached for
your review.

4. Should you wish additional information, you may contact (name
and rank of the designated point of contact) at (telephone
number).

5. Please provide a summary of your findings and recommendations
to me as soon as they are available.

                          (Signature)
                          Name of commanding officer

SAMPLE LETTER

SERVICEMEMBER NOTIFICATION OF COMMANDING OFFICER
REFERRAL FOR MENTAL HEALTH EVALUATION

FOR OFFICIAL USE ONLY

6320
Ser
Date

From: Commanding Officer, (Name of Command)
To: Commanding Officer, (Service member's rank, name and SSN)

Subj: NOTIFICATION OF COMMANDING OFFICER REFERRAL FOR MENTAL
        HEALTH EVALUATION (NON-EMERGENCY)

Ref: (a) DoD Directive 6490.1, "Mental Health Evaluations of
            Members of the Armed Forces," 1 Oct 97 (NOTAL)
        (b) SECNAV Instruction 6320.24A, "Requirements for Mental
            Health Evaluations of Members of the Armed Forces"
        (c) Section 546 of Public Law 102-484, "National Defense
            Authorization Act for Fiscal Year 1993," Oct 1992
        (d) DoD Directive 7050.6, "Military Whistleblower
            Protection," 12 Aug 95

1. Per references (a) through (d), this letter is to inform you
I am referring you for a mental health evaluation.

2. The following is a description of your behaviors and/or
verbal expressions I considered in determining the need for a
mental health evaluation: (Provide dates and a brief factual
description of the service member's actions of concern.)

3. Before making this referral, I consulted with the following
mental health care provider(s) about your recent actions: (list
rank, name, corps, branch of each provider consulted) at (name of
medical treatment facility (MTF) or clinic) on (date(s)).
(Rank(s) and name(s) of mental health care provider(s)) concur(s)
this evaluation is warranted and is appropriate.
                              OR
Consultation with a mental health care provider prior to this
referral is (was) not possible because (give reason; e.g.,
geographic isolation from available mental health care provider,
etc.)

FOR OFFICIAL USE ONLY

Enclosure (3)

FOR OFFICIAL USE ONLY

Subj: NOTIFICATION OF COMMANDING OFFICER REFERRAL FOR MENTAL
        HEALTH EVALUATION (NONEMERGENCY)

4.   Per references (a) and (b), you are entitled to the rights
listed below:

     a.   The right, upon your request, to speak with an attorney
who is a member of the Armed Forces or is employed by the
Department of Defense who is available for the purpose of
advising you of the ways in which you may seek redress should you
question this referral.

     b.   The right to submit to the DON Inspector General or to
the Department of Defense Inspector General (DoD IG) for
investigation, an allegation that your mental health evaluation
referral was in reprisal for making or attempting to make a
lawful communication to: a Member of Congress; any appropriate
authority in your chain of command; an IG; or a member of a DoD
audit, inspection, investigation or law enforcement organization.

     c.   The right to obtain a second medical opinion and be
evaluated by a mental health care provider of your own choosing,
at your own expense, if reasonably available. Such an evaluation
by an independent mental health care provider shall be conducted
within a reasonable period of time, usually within 10 business
days, and shall not delay nor substitute for an evaluation
performed by a DoD mental health care provider.

     d.   The right to communicate, without restriction, with an
IG, attorney, Member of Congress, or others about your referral
for a mental health evaluation. This provision does not apply to
a communication that is unlawful.

     e.   The right, except in emergencies, to have at least 2
business days before the scheduled mental health evaluation to
meet with an attorney, IG, chaplain, or other appropriate party.
If I believe your situation constitutes an emergency or your
condition appears potentially harmful to your well-being and I
judge it is not in your best interest to delay your mental health
evaluation for 2 business days, I shall state my reasons in
writing as part of the request for the mental health evaluation.

     f.   If you are assigned to a naval vessel, deployed or
otherwise geographically isolated because of circumstances
FOR OFFICIAL USE ONLY

Subj: NOTIFICATION OF COMMANDING OFFICER REFERRAL FOR MENTAL
HEALTH EVALUATION (NONEMERGENCY)

related to military duties that make compliance with any of the
procedures in paragraphs 3 and 4, impractical, I shall prepare
and give to you a copy of the letter setting forth the reasons
for my inability to comply with these procedures.

5. You are scheduled to meet with (name and rank of the mental
health care provider) at (name of MTF or clinic) on .(date) at
(time).

6. The following authorities can assist you if you wish to
question this referral:

    a. Military Attorney: (Provide location, telephone number
and available hours of nearest Naval Legal Service Office.)

    b. Inspector General: (Provide rank/title, name, address,
telephone number and available hours for service and DoD IG. The
DoD IG number is 1-800-424-9098.)

    c. Other available resources: (Provide rank, name
corps/title of chaplains or other resources available to counsel
and assist the service member.)

                    (Signature)
                    Name of commanding officer
I have read the letter above and have been provided a copy.
Service member's signature: _____
Date: _____

                        OR
The service member declined to sign this letter which includes
the service member's Statement of Rights because (give reason
and/or quote service member).

Witness's signature:_____
Date:_____

Witness's printed/typed rank and name:_____

_____

(Provide a copy of this letter to the service member.)

SAMPLE LETTER

FROM MENTAL HEALTH CARE PROVIDER
TO SERVICEMEMBER'S COMMANDING OFFICER

FOR OFFICIAL USE ONLY

6320
Ser
Date

From: (Rank and Name of Mental Health Care Provider)
To: Commanding Officer, (Service member's command)
Via: Commanding Officer, (Medical treatment facility or clinic)

Subj: MENTAL HEALTH EVALUATION IN THE CASE OF (SERVICE MEMBER'S
         RANK, NAME AND SSN)

Ref: (a) DoD Directive 6490.1, "Mental Health Evaluations of
             Members of the Armed Forces," 1 Oct 97
         (b) SECNAV Instruction 6320.24A, "Mental Health
             Evaluations of Members of the Armed Forces"

1. In compliance with references (a) and (b), the above named
service member was seen on (date) at (location) by (mental health
care provider's rank and name) after referral by (rank and name
of service member's commanding officer) for an emergency
evaluation because of (brief summary of pertinent facts)
                              OR
for a nonemergency command directed evaluation because of (brief
summary of pertinent facts).

2. The evaluation revealed (brief description of findings).

3. The Diagnosis(es) is/are

             Axis I
             Axis II
             Axis III

4. The servicemember is deemed unsuitable for continued
military Service on the basis of the above diagnosis(es).
(Provide explanation on how the service member's personality
disorder or substance abuse, for example, is maladaptive to
adequate performance of duty.)

FOR OFFICIAL USE ONLY

Enclosure (4)

Subj: MENTAL HEALTH EVALUATION IN THE CASE OF (SERVICE MEMBER'S
        RANK, NAME AND SSN)

5. This service member is considered (imminently dangerous or
potentially dangerous) based upon (summary of clinical data to
support this determination).

6. The following clinical treatment plan has been initiated:

    a. The service member has been admitted to (ward and name of
MTF or hospital) for further evaluation/observation/treatment.
His/her physician is (rank/title and name) who may be reached at
(telephone number).

                                OR

    b. The service member has been scheduled for outpatient
followup (or treatment) on (date and time) at (name of MTF or
mental health clinic) with (rank/title and name of privileged
mental health care provider) who may be reached at (telephone
number).

7. RECOMMENDATIONS TO THE COMMANDING OFFICER: The service
member is returned to his/her command, with the following
recommendations (for imminently or potentially dangerous service
members, only):

    a. Precautions: (e.g., order to move into military
barracks; prevent access to weapons; consider liberty/leave
restrictions; issue restraining order, etc.)
                              AND/OR
    b. Process for expeditious administrative separation per
applicable serve directive. The service member does not have a
severe mental disorder and is not considered mentally disordered;
however, he/she manifests a longstanding disorder of character,
behavior and adaptability that is of such severity to preclude
adequate military Service. Although not currently at significant
risk for suicide or homicide, due to his/her lifelong pattern of
maladaptive responses to routine personal and/or work-related
stressors, he/she may become dangerous to himself or herself or
others in the future.
                              AND/OR
    c. The servicemember (is/is not) suitable for continued
access to classified material and his/her (Secret/Top Secret/Top

FOR OFFICIAL USE ONLY

Subj: MENTAL HEALTH EVALUATION IN THE CASE OF (SERVICE MEMBER'S
RANK, NAME AND SSN)

Secret Special Compartmentalized Clearance) should be (retained/rescinded).

AND/OR

d. Other _____ (describe).

8. The above actions and recommendations have been discussed with the service member who acknowledged he/she understood them.
OR
The service member's condition (diagnosis(es)) prevent(s) him/her from understanding the actions taken and recommendations made above.

9. If you do not concur with these recommendations, reference (b) requires that you notify your next senior commanding officer within 2 business days explaining your decision to act against medical advice regarding administrative management of this service member.

(Signature)
Mental health care provider's
name, rank, corps, branch of
service

FOR OFFICIAL USE ONLY

GUIDELINES FOR MENTAL HEALTH EVALUATION
FOR IMMINENT DANGEROUSNESS

Clinical evaluations should include:

I. Record Review

   A. Medical Record

      1. History of pertinent medical problems and treatment
      2. History of substance abuse evaluations and/or treatment
      3. History of mental health evaluations and/or treatment

   B. Family Advocacy Program (if applicable)

   C. Service Personnel Record (if available)

   D. Review documentation for disciplinary problems and counseling

II. History

   A. History as obtained from the Service member and assessment of reliability

      1. History of past violence towards others: ("Have you ever hurt anyone physically? Who? What did you do? How badly was the person hurt? How did you feel about it afterward? How do you feel about it now?")

      2. Alcohol and illicit substance abuse/dependence

      3. Personal/marital problems

      4. Recent losses (job/family)

      5. Legal/financial problems

      6. History of childhood emotional, sexual and/or physical abuse or witnessing abuse

      7. Past psychiatric history

8. Past medical history and current/recent medications

B. Information from command representative on Service member's behavior, work performance and general functioning

C. Pertinent information from family or friends

III. Mental Status Examination (emphasis on abnormal presentation)

A. Appearance (ability to relate to the examiner, eye contact, hygiene, grooming)

B. Behavior (psychomotor agitation or retardation)

C. Speech (rate, rhythm)

D. Mood (service member's stated predominant mood)

E. Affect

F. Is examiner's observations of member's affect consistent with stated mood?

G. If inconsistent, in what way?

H. Thought Processes: Is there evidence of psychotic symptoms, paranoid thoughts or feelings?

I. Thought Content: What does the service member talk about spontaneously when allowed the opportunity? How does the service member respond to specific questions about the facts or issues which led to his/her psychological evaluation? Is there evidence of an irrational degree of anger, rage, jealousy?

J. Cognition: Is the service member oriented to person, place, time, date, and reason for the evaluation? Can he/she answer simple informational questions and do simple calculations?

K. Assessment of Suicide Potential:

1. Ideation: Do you have or have you had any thoughts about dying or hurting yourself?

2. Intent: Do you wish to die?

3. Plan: Will you hurt yourself or allow yourself to be hurt "accidentally or on purpose?" Do you have access to weapons at work or at home?

4. Behaviors: Have you taken any actions towards hurting yourself; for example, obtaining a weapon with which you could hurt yourself?

5. Attempts: Have you made prior suicide attempts? When? What did you do? How serious was the injury? Did you tell anyone? Did you want to die?

L. Assessment of Current Potential for Future Dangerous Behavior

1. Ideation: Do you have or have you recently had any thoughts to harm or kill anyone?

2. Intent: Do you wish anyone were injured or dead?

3. Plan: Will you hurt or try to kill anyone?

4. Behaviors: Have you verbally threatened to hurt or kill anyone? Have you obtained any weapons?

5. Attempts: Have you physically hurt anyone recently? (Describe.)

IV. Psychological Testing Results (if applicable)

V. Physical Examination and Laboratory Test Results (if applicable)

VI. Assessment Shall Include:

A. Axis I through III diagnoses, as indicated, and Axis IV and V assessments

B. A statement of clinical assessment of risk for dangerous behavior, supported by history obtained from the Service member and others, the mental status examination, pertinent actuarial factors and if pertinent, the physical examination and laboratory studies results.

VII. Recommendation/Plans Shall Address:

A. Further clinical evaluation and treatment, as indicated.

B. Precautions taken by the provider and recommendations to the service member's commanding officer.

C. Recommendations to the service member's commanding officer for administrative management.

VIII. Documentation

A. Documentation of the history, mental status examination, physical findings, assessment, and recommendations shall be recorded in the inpatient and outpatient record.

B. In those cases of individuals clinically judged to be imminently or potentially dangerous, a letter documenting the summary of clinical findings, precautions taken by the provider, verbal recommendations made to the service member's commanding officer, and current recommendations shall be forwarded by the mental health care provider via the medical treatment facility commanding officer to the Service member's commanding officer within 1 business day after the evaluation is completed. See enclosure (4).